T0064355

SECRETS
OF
CRIMINAL DEFENSE

by

Burton Milward, Jr.

authorHOUSE®

AuthorHouse™
1663 Liberty Drive
Bloomington, IN 47403
www.authorhouse.com
Phone: 1-800-839-8640

First published by AuthorHouse 4/25/2013

ISBN: 978-1-4678-4906-7 (sc)
ISBN: 978-1-4678-4907-4 (e)

Contents

Introduction

The excellent criminal defense attorney wins most of his cases.

He knows, somewhere in the lengthy process of criminal defense, the defense will get a break. He seizes that opportunity to achieve total victory.

The Total Victory Approach

The excellent criminal defense attorney lives and breathes total victory. He knows the terrain. He seizes every opportunity arising throughout the pretrial, trial, and posttrial process to achieve total victory.

He says, "I love the competition. I like to try cases against experienced prosecutors because I know their tricks, I know their angles, and I can get the better of them."

"The accused has a moral and legal right to have us on his side, to show his side, his defense, whatever it may be, so the jury has that before them as it considers its verdict. That's our job. Our life. Everything's against him except the presumption of innocence and the best defense. Only then does he get a square deal. You see that?"

— Earl Rogers, Los Angeles,
one of the greatest criminal
defense attorneys of all time

Secret 1 of Criminal Defense

The excellent criminal defense attorney's goal is total victory.

Secret 2 of Criminal Defense

Total victory is dismissal of the charge prior to trial, acquittal at trial, or reversal on appeal with directions to dismiss.

Secret 3 of Criminal Defense

A plea bargain is not total victory. A plea bargain appears to be a "win-win" situation, because the prosecution offers probation or a reduced sentence in exchange for a plea of guilty. *But the fact is the defendant loses when he enters a plea of guilty.*

Secret 4 of Criminal Defense

Total victory is not a "win-win" situation. Why should the prosecutor get anything? Total victory happens when the defense wins everything by dismissing the charge, obtaining acquittal, or setting aside a conviction on appeal.

Secret 5 of Criminal Defense

The excellent criminal defense attorney achieves the goal of total victory at any stage of a criminal prosecution. These stages include the investigation, pretrial motions, pretrial hearings, the trial, posttrial motions, the appeal, collateral attacks after conviction, or even the United States Supreme Court.

Secret 6 of Criminal Defense

In the investigation stage of a crime, the excellent criminal defense attorney advises his client to make no incriminating statements. The attorney may communicate an unbeatable defense to the prosecutor to convince the prosecutor not to file charges.

Secret 7 of Criminal Defense

The excellent criminal defense attorney achieves total victory by filing substantial pretrial motions to dismiss. These motions to dismiss include motions based on double jeopardy, equal protection, confrontation, speedy trial, failure to allege an essential element of the crime charged, and other recognized grounds. Any one of these is sufficient for the judge to enter an order dismissing the charge.

Plus, the excellent criminal defense attorney can always create other novel grounds for motions to dismiss based on the law.

Secret 8 of Criminal Defense

During the pretrial stage, the attorney files additional motions, such as motions to suppress — to limit the prosecutor's evidence at trial. Motions to suppress include motions to suppress statements made by the client, motions to suppress evidence seized from the client, motions to suppress a supposed identification of the client, and motions to otherwise limit evidence in the particular case.

Secret 9 of Criminal Defense

During the trial stage, the excellent criminal defense attorney achieves the goal of total victory by convincing the jury that the defendant has not been proven guilty beyond a reasonable doubt.

Secret 10 of Criminal Defense

If a client is convicted by the jury, the excellent criminal defense attorney files posttrial motions including: 1) a motion to arrest judgment based on grounds set forth in motions to dismiss; 2) a motion for judgment of acquittal notwithstanding the verdict of conviction, which shows that the crime charged was not proven beyond a reasonable doubt; and 3) a motion for new trial setting forth errors at trial which require a new trial. A new trial is not total victory, but it is a substantial step in that direction.

Secret 11 of Criminal Defense

If the jury convicts and the judge denies the defendant's posttrial motions and imposes a judgment and sentence, the excellent criminal defense attorney files an appeal to the next higher court and continues pursuing that appeal until relief is obtained.

Secret 12 of Criminal Defense

If a jury convicts the client, the trial court denies posttrial motions, the trial court imposes a judgment and sentence, and the court of appeals refuses to reverse the conviction, then the excellent criminal defense attorney seeks relief in the United States Supreme Court.

The United States Supreme Court is a defendant's ace in the hole. It's a long shot, but it can grant total victory. The excellent criminal defense attorney always seeks review by the United States Supreme Court.

Secret 13 of Criminal Defense

If the criminal defendant has not obtained relief after conviction and sentence, all the way through the United States Supreme Court, he is entitled to pursue postconviction collateral relief through a habeas corpus proceeding, also called a motion to vacate sentence. In this collateral attack, the excellent criminal defense attorney raises powerful constitutional issues, based on circumstances arising in the investigation, prosecution, trial, and appeal stages of the entire case, to set aside the judgment of conviction.

Constitutional Rights

The defendant is protected by constitutional rights that trump even the strongest evidence. When a defendant is charged in the criminal process, he is absolutely entitled to fundamental fairness and other specific aspects of due process. In our system, these constitutional protections prevail over laws, rules, facts, and opinion. The excellent criminal defense attorney applies these constitutional protections to win the defendant's case.

"The Constitution is the supreme law of the land. Our state and federal courts are duty bound to follow what it says. Use it to win your client's case."

— David E. Murrell, Louisville,
one of the greatest criminal
defense attorneys of all time

Secret 14 of Criminal Defense

Constitutional rights are the most powerful weapons in the excellent criminal defense attorney's arsenal.

These protections are guaranteed by the Bill of Rights in the United States Constitution. These rights are the foundation for all the laws and procedures that govern the criminal justice process.

The Fourth Amendment guarantees a citizen's right against unreasonable searches and seizures.

The Fifth Amendment guarantees protection against double jeopardy, a citizen's right to not stand trial twice for the same offense.

The Fifth Amendment guarantees protection against self-incrimination, a citizen's right to not be compelled to be a witness against himself.

The Fifth Amendment guarantees the right to due process of law, a citizen's right to fundamental fairness.

The Sixth Amendment guarantees a citizen's rights to a speedy trial and a public trial.

The Sixth Amendment guarantees a citizen's right to trial by jury.

The Sixth Amendment guarantees a citizen's right to be informed of the nature and cause of the accusation against him. This protection requires precise notification of the crime charged.

The Sixth Amendment guarantees a citizen's right to be confronted with the witnesses against him. This includes the right to cross-examine.

The Sixth Amendment guarantees a citizen's right to compulsory process for obtaining witnesses in his favor. This is the right to subpoena witnesses.

The Sixth Amendment guarantees a citizen's right to the assistance of counsel for his defense. This protection requires effective assistance of counsel.

The Eighth Amendment guarantees a citizen's right to reasonable bail. In other words, excessive bail shall not be imposed.

The Eighth Amendment also guarantees a citizen's right not to be subjected to cruel and unusual punishment.

Total Victory Pretrial Motions

The excellent criminal defense attorney files motions that win total victory by convincing the court to dismiss the charge.

"Tie your pretrial motions to the Constitution, especially the Bill of Rights, for criminal defendants. Interweave cold, hard facts into your motions. Facts and cases together make persuasive legal arguments."

— David E. Murrell, Louisville,
one of the greatest criminal
defense attorneys of all time

Secret 15 of Criminal Defense

The excellent criminal defense attorney files pretrial motions to dismiss the criminal charge, including motions to dismiss based on double jeopardy, selective enforcement, denial of the right of confrontation, failure to allege an essential element of the crime charged, speedy trial, and other creative grounds based on the law.

Secret 16 of Criminal Defense
— Double Jeopardy

The excellent criminal defense attorney files a pretrial motion to dismiss on the grounds of double jeopardy, in an appropriate case, based on the fact that the defendant has previously been put to trial on the charge he is accused of in the present indictment.

Secret 17 of Criminal Defense

— Selective Enforcement

The excellent criminal defense attorney files a pretrial motion to dismiss on the grounds of selective enforcement, in an appropriate case, based on the fact that the prosecutor's office has singled out one defendant among many citizens who could have been charged, all of whom were engaged in the same criminality. For instance, the prosecutor may choose to prosecute a Chinese restaurant owner but choose not to prosecute the American restaurant owner right next door, where both restaurants allegedly employ illegal immigrants. Such a prosecution denies the defendant's rights to due process and equal protection of the law guaranteed by the Fifth Amendment.

Secret 18 of Criminal Defense

— Denial of Right of Confrontation

The excellent criminal defense attorney files a pretrial motion to dismiss on the grounds of denial of the right of confrontation, in an appropriate case, based on the fact that the government has denied the defendant access to important witnesses, in violation of the Sixth Amendment. For instance, in an immigration case involving illegal restaurant workers, the government denied the defendant restaurant owner's right to confrontation by detaining illegal immigrant witnesses who incriminated the restaurant owner while deporting illegal immigrant witnesses who exonerated the restaurant owner.

Secret 19 of Criminal Defense

— Failure to Allege an Essential Element of the Crime

The excellent criminal defense attorney files a pretrial motion to dismiss on the grounds of failure to allege an essential element of the crime charged in the indictment, in an appropriate case, based on the requirement that the defendant must be given specific notice of the charge against him. The Sixth Amendment to the Constitution guarantees that an accused person shall "be informed of the nature and cause of the accusation." If this requirement is not met, the charge must be dismissed.

Secret 20 of Criminal Defense

— Speedy Trial

The excellent criminal defense attorney files a pretrial motion to dismiss on the grounds of denial of speedy trial, in an appropriate case, based on the fact that the prosecutor brought a charge and then failed to prosecute it within a reasonable time, denying the defendant's Sixth Amendment right to a speedy trial.

Secret 21 of Criminal Defense
— Other Creative Grounds for Dismissal

The excellent criminal defense attorney has all the law, all the cases, and all the rules of procedure at his fingertips. Out of these tools, he creates new, invincible motions to dismiss.

Secret 22 of Criminal Defense
— Example of Creative Grounds for Dismissal

The excellent criminal defense attorney created a novel motion to dismiss a federal indictment. His motion was denied prior to trial, denied at trial, denied posttrial, and failed on appeal, but was granted by the United States Supreme Court.

The attorney's creative motion was based on the theory that intangible-right-to-honest-government fraud was not within the scope of the mail fraud statute. The United States Supreme Court held the mail fraud statute applied only to tangible rights, such as property or money, not to the intangible right to honest government. In *United States v. McNally*, 483 U.S. 350 (1987), the United States Supreme Court upheld the attorney's motion and ordered dismissal of the indictment.

The excellent criminal defense attorney takes the time to work through the laws, cases, and rules to create substantial, new motions to dismiss.

Additional Pretrial Motions

The excellent criminal defense attorney files additional pretrial motions that do not win the entire case by dismissing the charge, but instead convince the court to: 1) require the prosecution to disclose information about its evidence prior to trial, and 2) limit or exclude the prosecution's evidence at trial.

"Cases are won before you ever get to the courtroom."

— Frank E. Haddad, Jr.,
former President of the National
Association of Criminal
Defense Lawyers

Secret 23 of Criminal Defense

The excellent criminal defense attorney files additional pretrial motions in almost every criminal prosecution, including: motion for discovery, motion for bill of particulars, motion to disclose deals with witnesses, motion for disclosure of informants, and motion for grand jury testimony. In most cases, the trial judge orders the prosecutor to reveal the requested information prior to trial. Disclosure avoids delay during trial, and helps both sides prepare for trial.

The excellent criminal defense attorney also files motions to suppress to exclude evidence obtained by the government in violation of constitutional rights, including: motion to suppress based on an unreasonable search and seizure, motion to suppress based on an involuntary statement by the defendant, and motion to suppress based on an unreliable or suggestive identification of the defendant.

In a particular case, the excellent criminal defense attorney may file a special pretrial motion, such as a motion for change of venue.

Secret 24 of Criminal Defense

The pretrial motion for discovery seeks disclosure prior to trial of physical evidence such as photographs or recordings or expert witness reports or any scientific test results obtained by the prosecution. The trial court orders the prosecution to make these disclosures prior to trial as a matter of course.

Secret 25 of Criminal Defense

The pretrial motion for a bill of particulars is based on the failure of the indictment to specifically notify the defendant of the charge against him. In the motion for a bill of particulars, the excellent criminal defense attorney requests precise details: where did the crime occur, when did the crime occur, and how did the crime occur? The trial court orders the prosecutor to provide these particulars to assure the defendant has notice of the specific charge against him, as required by state and federal constitutions.

Secret 26 of Criminal Defense

The pretrial motion to disclose deals with witnesses requests specific information about the prosecutor's promises to witnesses in exchange for testimony incriminating the defendant.

For instance, a prosecution witness is charged with a crime, usually a crime related to the charge against the defendant. The prosecutor offers the witness a deal. The prosecutor says, "Now, look here, Mr. Bell, you're facing twenty years in prison and a $100,000 fine. You don't want to serve all that time or pay all that money. I'll make you an offer. I'll allow you to plead guilty to a lesser charge and pay a one-hundred dollar fine only, if you'll testify against this defendant so we can convict him. What do you say?" The witness agrees to the deal and testifies in the way the prosecutor and the police tell him to testify.

Because the defendant, represented by the excellent criminal defense attorney, has the right to cross-examine witnesses against him, the court orders the prosecutor to disclose deals with prosecution witnesses.

Secret 27 of Criminal Defense

Often, in the investigation of a case, or the creation of a crime, the prosecution and police use undercover informants wired with a transmitter or recording device. These informants buy drugs from, or help, the defendant in some crime.

The excellent criminal defense attorney requests the court to order the prosecutor to disclose the identity of these informants prior to trial because the defendant is entitled to confront witnesses against him, and because these informants are material witnesses to the crime charged. This request is resisted by the prosecutor, who says the defendant will harm these informants for betraying him.

Nevertheless, the excellent criminal defense attorney argues the trial judge should order disclosure prior to trial, to help the defense prepare for trial and avoid delay at trial.

Secret 28 of Criminal Defense

The pretrial motion for grand jury testimony requests the court to order the prosecutor to disclose prior to trial the grand jury testimony of witnesses who will be testifying at trial. These transcripts provide a preview of details of the prosecution's theory and evidence. Even if not disclosed prior to trial, the grand jury testimony of a witness must be disclosed during trial, to assure meaningful confrontation.

The testimony of the defendant before the grand jury is a statement of the defendant, which is always disclosed prior to trial.

Secret 29 of Criminal Defense

The pretrial motion to suppress evidence seized in an unlawful search is based on the federal constitutional Fourth Amendment prohibition against "unreasonable searches and seizures," or a parallel state constitutional guarantee. The search and seizure component of criminal practice is an ever-evolving part of the law. The excellent criminal defense attorney stays current with this area of law so that his practice techniques remain state-of-the-art.

Secret 30 of Criminal Defense

The pretrial motion to suppress unreliable or suggestive identification evidence is based on the constitutional Fifth Amendment provision that guarantees a defendant the right to "due process of law," or a parallel state constitutional guarantee. Due process is fundamental fairness in the application of the criminal process to a suspect or defendant. In attacking an identification as unreliable, the excellent criminal defense attorney attacks the various contexts of identification which may be suggestive, such as: a line-up, an individual show-up, a photographic identification, or a video identification.

The excellent criminal defense attorney may retain an identification-evidence expert to help prepare and present his motion.

Secret 31 of Criminal Defense

The pretrial motion to suppress involuntary statements attributed to the defendant is based on the Fifth Amendment guarantee that no person shall be "compelled in any criminal case to be a witness against himself" and the Sixth Amendment guarantee of "the assistance of counsel," or parallel state constitutional guarantees. For example, the police may have arrested an individual and hit him with a rubber hose until he confessed to a crime. In such a case, the confession, or statement, is a constitutionally prohibited "compelled" self-incriminating statement, rather than a freely given statement, and must be suppressed.

Secret 32 of Criminal Defense

The excellent criminal defense attorney files a pretrial motion for change of venue when he believes the defendant cannot receive a fair trial in the community where the trial is scheduled. Prejudicial pretrial publicity may adversely depict the defendant as some kind of a demon, the community may dislike the defendant's family, or the defendant may have a bad reputation in the community.

The excellent criminal defense attorney obtains change of venue by hiring professors in the sociology department at a nearby university to take a survey to demonstrate that the defendant cannot get a fair trial in the community.

These professors manufacture the kind of survey they want. They formulate helpful questions. They conduct a survey of the residents in the community and write helpful conclusions. These professors testify as experts in their field. Their end product persuades the court to grant the motion to change venue.

Federal or state prosecutors seldom seriously oppose a pretrial motion to change venue based on a well-conceived, scholarly survey.

Trial Preparation

Trial preparation is everything to the excellent criminal defense attorney. He has seen the entire process come and go many times; he knows where the opportunities are. He works with the defendant to do everything they can think of, within the rules and ethical standards, to 1) minimize or eliminate the prosecutor's case, and 2) maximize the presentation of the defense theory to the jury.

"I prepare. I leave no stone unturned."

— Richard "Racehorse" Haynes,
Houston, one of the greatest
criminal defense attorneys
of all time

Secret 33 of Criminal Defense

In preparing for trial, the excellent criminal defense attorney understands he has no duty whatsoever to prove the defendant is not guilty. The prosecutor has the duty to prove the guilt of a criminal defendant, as charged, beyond a reasonable doubt.

Secret 34 of Criminal Defense

The excellent criminal defense attorney prepares to make the lesser argument defeat the greater argument, even where his client has perhaps forty percent of the truth, while the prosecution has perhaps sixty percent of the truth.

The prosecutor may begin with the upper hand, but the excellent criminal defense attorney works harder and conducts more thorough preparation than the prosecution. He gives closer attention to detail. He prepares to present a superior case with witnesses and exhibits. The jury will see the defense theory more clearly than the prosecution theory.

The excellent criminal defense attorney presents more precise legal authorities regarding the admission or exclusion of evidence at trial, to minimize the prosecution's evidence. He prepares to submit straightforward jury instructions to the court.

His demeanor will be friendlier and more courteous with jurors and court personnel during trial. His jury selection will be better informed. His closing argument will be more persuasive than the prosecution's closing argument.

Secret 35 of Criminal Defense

The excellent criminal defense attorney understands that prosecutors like to charge criminal conspiracy. The only evidence needed to demonstrate conspiracy is an agreement between two or more people and one overt act in furtherance of the conspiracy. An overt act can be as simple as a telephone conversation, or a trip into town, which the prosecutor claims is "in furtherance of the conspiracy." Conspiracy is easy to prove.

The excellent criminal defense attorney knows how to turn the tables on a prosecutor's conspiracy charge. For instance, in a federal extortion case, where a defendant-politician is charged with conspiracy to extort campaign contributions from a road contractor in exchange for granting road-building contracts to the contractor, the excellent criminal defense attorney shows the only conspiracy committed, if any, is the road contractor's conspiracy to bribe the defendant-politician in exchange for road-building contracts.

When the excellent criminal defense attorney demonstrates a conspiracy to commit bribery, not extortion, the charge of conspiracy to commit extortion against his client must be either dismissed or acquitted.

Secret 36 of Criminal Defense

In a particular case, when the excellent criminal defense attorney wants to prepare a mental defense, the defendant resists. He says, "Lawyer, I'm not insane. Do I look insane to you? I don't need any tests."

The attorney convinces the defendant to undergo psychological tests by saying, "You and I both know you're not insane. Let's put an end to this insanity talk once and for all. Just go over there and take all these tests and prove you're not insane. Will you help me with that?"

To demonstrate to the world that he is *not* insane, the defendant agrees to go. He undergoes the psychological testing. When the results come back, the defendant is certified insane, and the excellent criminal defense attorney presents a substantial and credible mental defense.

Secret 37 of Criminal Defense

The excellent criminal defense attorney deals with pretrial publicity by continuing to thoroughly prepare for trial.

In high-profile cases, the prosecutor leaks damaging information to the news media in hopes of swaying public opinion against the defendant. News media outlets pick up these leaks and broadcast them. Undeterred, the excellent criminal defense attorney and his defendant go about their business of preparing to demolish the prosecutor's case at trial. They prepare the presentation of their theory of defense. They know the battle will be won at trial, not in the media.

Total Victory Trial Tools

At trial, the excellent criminal defense attorney wields powerful tools to achieve total victory. These tools include the presumption of innocence, the rule of law that the indictment is not evidence of guilt, the rule of reasonable doubt, his reminder to the jury that it has the power of God over the future of his client, his rapport with the trial jury, and repeated requests for acquittal.

"In America, a criminal trial is not about guilt or innocence. It's about whether the prosecution can prove the charge beyond a reasonable doubt."

— Frank E. Haddad, Jr.,
former President of the National
Association of Criminal
Defense Lawyers

Secret 38 of Criminal Defense

The excellent criminal defense attorney always educates jurors about the presumption of innocence. During jury selection, the attorney asks each juror if he believes in the presumption of innocence, that the defendant begins the case with a clean slate, and that the prosecution has the burden to prove guilt beyond a reasonable doubt. The attorney asks, "Will you follow that law?"

In his opening statement, the excellent criminal defense attorney reminds jurors they promised to follow the rule of presumption of innocence.

Again, after all the evidence has been introduced, the trial judge instructs jurors that the defendant is presumed to be innocent and that the prosecution has the burden of proof.

Finally, in closing argument, the excellent criminal defense attorney says, "And another thing that the judge told you and all of us, and you agreed to when you were being selected as jurors in this case, was that the defendant was entitled to the presumption of innocence in this country, so this defendant is entitled to be presumed innocent in this country."

Through all these stages of the trial — jury selection, opening statement, trial judge's instructions, and defense closing argument — the excellent criminal defense attorney educates the jury about the presumption of innocence.

Secret 39 of Criminal Defense

During jury selection, the excellent criminal defense attorney always educates jurors about the importance of the rule of law that the indictment is not evidence of guilt. He asks each juror to follow this rule.

He reminds jurors of this rule again in his opening statement and in his closing argument. He states in closing, "The judge told you early on, before you were selected as a juror, that the indictment was not evidence in this case. It wasn't to be considered by you as evidence in this case. An indictment is just a sheet of paper, or sheets of paper, that has written down on it what the charge is. It's not evidence of anything. And the fact is an indictment is merely the paper by which this court says that a person is charged. No evidence against anybody."

Secret 40 of Criminal Defense

During jury selection, the excellent criminal defense attorney always educates jurors about the important rule that the burden is on prosecutors to prove beyond a reasonable doubt that the defendant is guilty of the offense charged. If the prosecution fails to prove guilt beyond a reasonable doubt, then jurors must return a verdict of not guilty. Each of the jurors agrees to follow this rule.

In his opening statement, the excellent criminal defense attorney reminds jurors that the prosecution has the burden of proving guilt beyond a reasonable doubt.

In its instructions, the trial court states the rule that the prosecution has the burden to prove every essential element of the crime charged against the defendant beyond a reasonable doubt, and that if the prosecution fails to meet its burden, then jurors must acquit the defendant.

In his closing argument, the excellent criminal defense attorney reminds jurors of the vast importance of the rule of reasonable doubt. "The instruction that you've been given on reasonable doubt from the judge is given in every case that's tried in the United States where somebody has been charged with a violation of the law."

In closing argument, the excellent criminal defense attorney states, "The burden is always upon the prosecution to prove guilt beyond a reasonable doubt. So if the jurors, you jurors sitting here, after a careful and impartial consideration of all the evidence, have a reasonable doubt that the defendant is guilty of the charge, you must find the defendant not guilty. That is the instruction of the court, that is the rule of law, and you promised me during jury selection that you would follow that rule of law, and I ask you to do so and acquit this defendant."

By the time the jury has heard about the rule of reasonable doubt during jury selection, in the defense opening statement, in the trial court's instructions, and in the defense closing argument, the jury is thoroughly educated about the rule of reasonable doubt, and well aware of its power to acquit.

Secret 41 of Criminal Defense

At trial, the power of the jury is absolute.

Each juror has a vote to acquit or convict. Their verdict must be unanimous. The excellent criminal defense attorney characterizes the jury's power during closing argument.

"Today is an important day for us. But, really, it's the most important day in the life of this defendant. His life will be in your hands very shortly. All of us, ladies and gentlemen, from time to time have wished we had divine power of some kind. You will have that divine power when you retire to your jury room in this case. Everything that is dear to this man will be in your hands. You will have the power of God to determine what will be his future in this case."

This power was demonstrated in the O.J. Simpson and Casey Anthony murder trials.

Secret 42 of Criminal Defense

Throughout trial, the excellent criminal defense attorney projects a polite, sincere demeanor toward the court, prosecuting attorneys, each and every witness testifying, all of the court personnel, and jurors. The attorney stands up to the prosecution and projects his firm resolve to defend his client, so that jurors can conclude they would want this attorney to represent them, if they were ever accused of a crime.

Often, if jurors like the defense attorney, they will acquit the defendant on that basis alone.

Secret 43 of Criminal Defense

During trial, the excellent criminal defense attorney has repeated opportunities to ask for a judgment of acquittal.

After the prosecution completes putting on its evidence, the attorney requests the court to enter a judgment of acquittal because the prosecution's proof is insufficient to prove the charge alleged. If the trial judge denies that motion for acquittal, then the defense puts on its proof.

After the attorney puts on the defense evidence, he again requests the judge to grant acquittal on the grounds that *all* the evidence introduced is insufficient to prove the alleged crime beyond a reasonable doubt. If the trial judge denies that motion for acquittal, then the case goes to the jury.

During closing argument, the excellent criminal defense attorney asks jurors to return a verdict of acquittal.

Secret 44 of Criminal Defense

The single most important factor in obtaining the total victory of acquittal at trial is to stand up for the client. The excellent criminal defense attorney does not back down. He says: "They may knock us out of the ring, but they will not scare us out of the ring."

Additional Trial Tools

The excellent criminal defense attorney makes the constitutional guarantee of a fair trial come alive in the courtroom. He makes the ideal of fairness tangible and visible, during jury selection, cross-examination, defense evidence and instructions, and closing argument.

He uses all the tools at his disposal.

"Give me a new, fresh jury, and I will win 99% of the time."

— Frank E. Haddad, Jr.,
former President of the National
Association of Criminal
Defense Lawyers

Secret 45 of Criminal Defense

During selection of the jury, the excellent criminal defense attorney questions prospective jurors personally to determine if he wants them on the jury, or the trial judge may conduct personal examinations of each juror, based on questions provided by the defense attorney and the prosecutor.

The attorney asks each prospective juror if he understands the presumption of innocence, if he believes in the presumption of innocence, and if he will follow that principle of law when he sits as a juror. He asks each prospective juror to answer yes or no. He also asks each prospective juror about the rule of reasonable doubt, and the principle of law that the indictment is but a piece of paper upon which the charge is written and not proof of guilt in any way, and whether each prospective juror agrees with these principles.

In selecting the jury, the excellent criminal defense attorney strikes intelligent professionals like engineers from the jury because they tend to be conservative leaders prone to convince jurors to convict. The attorney prefers to keep ordinary, good-hearted men and women, comfortable with themselves, who tend to give a defendant the benefit of any doubt and return a verdict of not guilty.

Secret 46 of Criminal Defense

The defendant is entitled to a jury trial, or the defendant can waive his right to a jury trial and be tried by a judge.

When the excellent criminal defense attorney faces the decision whether to try the case before a jury or before the judge, he knows a jury is unpredictable and can return any verdict it wants. However, the attorney may also know that the judge assigned to try the case has a track record of leniency with regard to the charge being prosecuted, with regard to defendants in general, or with regard to defendants with the same background as his client.

The excellent criminal defense attorney uses his best judgment to select either a jury or the judge to try the case, based on a single factor — whether the judge or a jury will acquit his defendant.

Secret 47 of Criminal Defense

The excellent criminal defense attorney knows which defenses he can present to the jury.

The alibi defense demonstrates the defendant could not have been present at the time or location of the alleged crime because he was somewhere else, so he could not have committed the crime.

The defense of self-defense demonstrates the death of the deceased was the fault of the deceased, who attacked the defendant, forcing the defendant to protect himself.

The defense-of-another defense demonstrates the deceased was attacking another person, such as the defendant's family or a police officer, with deadly force, so the defendant was justified in taking the life of the deceased.

The defense of justification demonstrates that, although the defendant committed the offense alleged, he was justified in doing so.

The defense of impossibility demonstrates that it would be impossible for the defendant to have committed the offense. For instance the defendant has a serious angina heart condition, which makes it impossible for him to commit the strenuous crime alleged.

A mental defense, such as the defense of insanity, demonstrates that the defendant was so insane that he lacked the required criminal intent to commit the crime charged.

The excellent criminal defense attorney may present a once-only defense, such as: "the S.O.B. deserved it"; or "the defendant was awarded a silver star in Vietnam."

Secret 48 of Criminal Defense

The Fifth Amendment to the United States Constitution guarantees a criminal defendant's right to not testify at trial. A defendant who chooses not to testify cannot be forced to testify by the trial judge.

The excellent criminal defense attorney knows that when a defendant chooses not to testify, the Fifth Amendment prohibits the prosecutor or the trial judge from making any adverse comment during the trial about the defendant's decision not to testify. The attorney makes sure the trial judge instructs jurors that no inference of guilt may be drawn from the defendant's decision not to testify.

Secret 49 of Criminal Defense

The "guilty" client who demands his right to a trial is not a problem for the experienced criminal defense attorney.

The attorney is perfectly willing and ethically correct to proceed to represent the defendant at trial, to obtain acquittal, or to ensure that the defendant is not convicted unless and until the prosecutor presents proof beyond a reasonable doubt demonstrating guilt in a fair proceeding. The attorney earns his fee when he shoulders the responsibility to guarantee the defendant receives a fair trial.

Secret 50 of Criminal Defense

When a "guilty" client demands his right to testify at trial, the excellent criminal defense attorney allows the client to testify.

The excellent criminal defense attorney does *not* examine the "guilty" client on the stand, perhaps eliciting false testimony, which would be unethical. But the attorney, within the rules, advises the court and jurors that the defendant wishes to take the stand and make a statement. The attorney introduces his client and states, "My client wishes to make a statement under oath, but I will not be examining him." Then the defendant testifies with his statement.

This is a dangerous situation, because the defendant's testimony is subject to cross-examination. Few "guilty" clients can withstand cross-examination by a prosecutor without tripping over their own falsehoods, or providing incriminating evidence, leading to devastating consequences for the defense.

The best way to deal with a "guilty" client is to counsel the client not to testify at all. A criminal defendant has the absolute right not to testify at trial, and this is often the best course. The excellent criminal defense attorney can still win at trial, even where his client does not testify.

Secret 51 of Criminal Defense

When his own defendant is afraid to testify, the excellent criminal defense attorney works with the defendant until he is able to testify, even though it takes a lot of time and understanding. The defendant is able to establish the defense theory of the case.

Secret 52 of Criminal Defense

When a prosecution witness is afraid to testify on cross-examination, the excellent criminal defense attorney argues that the defendant is unable to confront the witness against him, as guaranteed by the constitution, so that the charge must be dismissed.

Secret 53 of Criminal Defense

The excellent criminal defense attorney cross-examines the prosecution witness who has made a deal for leniency in exchange for testimony against the defendant.

The attorney asks how much incarceration the witness faced under the charges against him before the deal, how much of a fine the witness faced before the deal, and the details of the deal. "Was the deal an exchange of prison time for testimony?" "How much time did you spend in jail before you made the deal?" "Has the prosecutor promised to dismiss the charges against you after you testify?"

The excellent criminal defense attorney determines whether objective evidence corroborates the witness' testimony, or whether the testimony is an unbelievable fabrication. "Were you released from jail after the deal was made?" "Can we see a copy of the written contract here in court?" The attorney requests the writing be circulated to the jury. The attorney asks whether the witness testified before the grand jury. "May I examine the transcript of that grand jury testimony, please?" He attacks variations in the witness' testimony, then and now.

In closing argument, the excellent criminal defense attorney states that the prosecution is aware its witness is a habitual criminal, a persistent offender, a liar; that the prosecution released its witness from jail in exchange for the promise of testimony against the defendant; and that the prosecution wants the defendant to be convicted and sent to the penitentiary on the testimony of this kind of scum.

The excellent criminal defense attorney cautions the jurors it would be a miscarriage of justice to base a verdict of guilty on the testimony of this prosecution witness. The attorney asks the jurors point blank, "How horrible would it be to go through life thinking that you have voted a guilty verdict for a person who really wasn't guilty, based on the false testimony of this prosecution witness whose testimony has been bought with a promise of leniency?"

Secret 54 of Criminal Defense

The excellent criminal defense attorney successfully cross-examines the prosecution's expert witness. The prosecution's expert witness is on the payroll of the police department or the FBI, has one or more Ph.D. degrees, uses state-of-the-art equipment, and attends witness school to polish his presentation.

This prosecution's expert witness testifies, for instance, that there is a match between Substance A and Substance B that links the defendant to the crime.

The excellent criminal defense attorney asks, "Now, Professor Smith, you are here testifying for the prosecution, are you not?"

"Yes, counsel, I am."

"And you are testifying as an expert, are you not?"

"Yes, I'm testifying as an expert."

"And the court has qualified you as an expert witness, has it not?"

"Yes, it has."

"So, you are permitted by the court to give your expert opinion, are you not?"

"Yes, I am."

"And really what you have testified to here is your opinion, is it not?"

"Yes, this is my opinion."

"And you will agree, will you not, sir, that where there is an opinion, there can be differences of opinion?"

"Yes, there can be differences of opinion."

"So it's very possible, is it not, that someone could disagree with *your* opinion?"

"Yes, that's possible."

"So, what you're saying, Professor Smith, is that the defense in this case could very well bring in its own expert witness who could disagree with your opinion?"

"Yes."

Later in the trial, when the excellent criminal defense attorney calls his expert, the jury already understands the prosecution's expert testimony is just an opinion, and that the defense expert's opinion that there is no match between Substance A and Substance B, so that the defendant is not linked to the crime, is worthy of consideration.

Secret 55 of Criminal Defense

When the excellent criminal defense attorney cross-examines a prosecution witness, he is not able to write down the witness' answers because he is asking the questions. Nevertheless, the excellent criminal defense attorney keeps track of these answers.

In a long trial, the attorney requests the court reporter to provide daily transcripts of the witness' testimony, or important parts of the testimony. Another technique to keep track of a witness' answers during cross-examination is to have the attorney's trial assistant write down his questions and the witness' answers.

The excellent criminal defense attorney uses these answers during closing argument, when he quotes verbatim the prosecution's own witnesses' helpful statements, to establish the defense theory of the case.

Secret 56 of Criminal Defense

The excellent criminal defense attorney is always alert to prosecutorial or police misconduct, which causes a mistrial. When something happens *at trial* to deny a fair trial — something so prejudicial that it corrupts the trial completely — a mistrial is declared.

For instance, if the prosecutor makes an adverse comment at trial about the defendant's decision not to testify, then that comment destroys the fairness of the whole trial. In another instance, if a police officer testifies at trial that the defendant failed three polygraph examinations, it destroys the fairness of the whole trial because polygraph results are unreliable under the law, and references to them are not permitted.

When the court declares a mistrial, the case is set for retrial at a later date. However, if the prosecutor intentionally corrupts the trial, the excellent criminal defense attorney asks the court to rule the double-jeopardy clause of the constitution protects the defendant from any further retrial.

Secret 57 of Criminal Defense

The excellent criminal defense attorney uses character witnesses to demonstrate the defendant is a good person.

The jurors do not know the defendant, so the attorney calls witnesses who know the defendant. The attorney asks the character witness, "What is the defendant's reputation for truthfulness and honesty in the community?" The character witness testifies the defendant's reputation for truthfulness and honesty in the community is excellent. The attorney asks the character witness, "What is the defendant's reputation for being a law-abiding citizen in the community?" The character witness testifies the defendant's reputation for being a law-abiding citizen in the community is excellent.

When the prosecutor cross-examines the defense character witness, he asks, "Now, Mr. Johnson, you have testified that the defendant's reputation for truthfulness is excellent, and you have testified that his reputation for being a law-abiding citizen is excellent. Now, does the fact that the defendant is charged with the crime of murder change your opinion that he is an honest and law-abiding man?"

The excellent criminal defense attorney has prepared his character witness to answer, "No, my opinion is not changed. The defendant is an honest man of high integrity, very law-abiding, and it would have to be proven to me *beyond a reasonable doubt* that he committed the crime charged!"

Secret 58 of Criminal Defense

The excellent criminal defense attorney deals openly and fearlessly with trial publicity.

He treats media outlets, and therefore the public, much as he treats the jury. He states with authority, "The procedure in a trial requires the prosecution to put on its evidence first. The prosecution's evidence in this case is weak. But, even so, let's keep an open mind until we hear *all* the evidence. No one should conclude the defendant's guilt or innocence until *all* the evidence is heard. We will present the defendant's theory of the case."

He answers media questions directly, and states the defense theory in his answers. "Ultimately, we hope to prevail when the jury hears our evidence and decides to acquit this accused citizen of our community."

When news media outlets want to take photographs of the defendant and the defendant's family, the excellent criminal defense attorney sends the defendant's family around to a side door into the courthouse, but presents the defendant dressed up nice and smiling for the cameras. "We look forward to vindicating the good name of this outstanding citizen. Thank you."

Secret 59 of Criminal Defense

When the excellent criminal defense attorney tries a case out of town, he employs tactics to improve his chances for total victory.

He retains an attorney from the community where the trial is being held to assist the defense. This local counsel is a lawyer of good reputation in the community, who sits at the defense table with the excellent criminal defense attorney and the defendant during the whole trial. This local counsel provides substantial help with the selection of the jury. He knows potential jurors, and he knows which ones to keep who will likely acquit the defendant. He is friendly with these potential jurors.

In addition, the excellent criminal defense attorney establishes a base of operations at a local law firm. This may be the local counsel's law firm, or it may be another law firm. This gives the attorney a place to rest and regroup, where he communicates with the people he needs to communicate with, and where he prepares witnesses or does whatever it takes to prepare for the next day of trial. At this base of operations, the defense attorney uses all the resources of the law office, including the law library, the computers and printers, and the advice of trial lawyers in the firm.

The excellent criminal defense attorney is not at a disadvantage when trying a case out of town; he marshals these resources.

Secret 60 of Criminal Defense

In his opening statement, the excellent criminal defense attorney requests jurors to keep their minds open throughout the prosecution's evidence and to listen carefully to the defense evidence, before making up their minds. Most jurors keep an open mind throughout the trial in anticipation of the lawyers' closing arguments.

In closing argument, the excellent criminal defense attorney asks the jury to make up their minds in favor of the defendant, to vote for a verdict of not guilty.

Secret 61 of Criminal Defense

The main points in the excellent criminal defense attorney's closing argument to the jury include the following:

He warmly greets the jury.

He thanks jurors for their close attention.

He states the purpose of closing argument is to summarize the facts and the law in the case.

He reminds jurors that the indictment is not evidence.

He reminds jurors of the presumption of innocence.

He reminds jurors of the rule of reasonable doubt.

He reminds jurors that they agreed to follow these rules of law.

He reviews the evidence at length. He argues any and all points, which naturally flow from the facts and law, in favor of the defense theory.

He points out ways in which the defense evidence is believable and the prosecution's evidence is not believable.

He outlines in detail the reasonable doubts in this particular case.

He appeals to jurors' sympathy for the defendant.

He reminds jurors of their absolute power over the defendant's future.

He requests jurors to return a verdict of not guilty.

He warmly appreciates and thanks jurors for their close attention throughout the trial.

Secret 62 of Criminal Defense

In a proper case, the excellent criminal defense attorney asks the jury to ignore the judge's instructions concerning the law and decide the case in accordance with its own idea of justice. This is the jury nullification argument, in which jurors agree the crime charged is on the books, and the defendant is guilty as charged, but they vote to nullify the law as applied to this particular defendant in this particular trial.

Jury nullification is well established in Anglo-American jurisprudence. In 1670, an English jury acquitted William Penn, even though he was guilty of preaching a Quaker sermon. The highest court in England ruled that jurors have a right to nullify the law. In 1735, an American jury acquitted John Peter Zenger, a newspaper publisher, even though he was proven guilty of seditious libel against the English governor of New York. The United States Supreme Court's decision in *Sparf v. United States,* 156 U.S. 51 (1895), upheld jury nullification.

Juries exercise their power of jury nullification in cases involving moral issues, such as draft protests, war protests, nuclear armament protests, protests for or against abortion, and the making of illegal whiskey during prohibition.

The excellent criminal defense attorney understands that, while the trial judge has no duty to instruct jurors about their power to exercise jury nullification, he can argue jury nullification on behalf of his defendant. Jury nullification is yet another technique to achieve the total victory of acquittal.

Secret 63 of Criminal Defense

In a criminal trial, the jury verdict must be unanimous. All of the jurors must vote to convict, or all of the jurors must vote to acquit. The excellent criminal defense attorney benefits greatly from this rule, and always aims for a unanimous verdict of acquittal.

Secret 64 of Criminal Defense

When the case goes to the jury, the defendant asks, "What will the jury do?" Another defendant might ask, "How long will they be out?"

The excellent criminal defense attorney answers, "Que sera, sera, whatever will be, will be."

Secret 65 of Criminal Defense

The excellent criminal defense attorney knows that jurors know they have absolute power to acquit or convict the defendant, that jurors are completely unpredictable, and that they will do what they want to do.

When the jury returns with its verdict, the attorney is on the edge of his chair just like the defendant.

Secret 66 of Criminal Defense

A trial jury's verdict of acquittal satisfies the excellent criminal defense attorney. He actually helps a person, earns his fee, and wins the battle in a fair fight. He achieves total victory.

A jury acquittal empowers. The judge announces, "Mr. Smith, you are a free man."

An acquittal clears the attorney's desk. He organizes and closes the file. He turns his thoughts, energy, and resources to his next case.

Secret 67 of Criminal Defense

The trial judge cannot overrule a verdict of acquittal. In the case of an acquittal, the jury's verdict is final.

However, a judge can overrule a verdict of guilty. If the jury returns a verdict of guilty, the excellent criminal defense attorney requests the judge to rule as a matter of law that there was insufficient evidence to support the verdict, in which case the judge's determination of insufficient evidence would be a final judgment of acquittal.

Secret 68 of Criminal Defense

In the event that the jury convicts, the excellent criminal defense attorney files a creative posttrial motion for acquittal.

One example of a successful posttrial motion for acquittal occurred in the case of *United States v. Bronston*, 409 U.S. 352 (1973), where the prosecution obtained a conviction for perjury.

In *Bronston*, the excellent criminal defense attorney analyzed the perjury statute and concluded the prosecution should not have prosecuted his client for giving an evasive or unresponsive answer under oath, which was literally true. He filed a posttrial motion after conviction.

Many months later, the United States Supreme Court unanimously held that giving an evasive or unresponsive answer to a question was not conduct that violated the perjury statute, so long as the answer was literally true. The Supreme Court reasoned that, "if a witness evades, it is the [prosecutor's] responsibility to recognize the evasion and to bring the witness back to the mark, to flush out the whole truth with the tools of adversary examination." The Supreme Court ordered the perjury conviction set aside and the indictment dismissed.

The excellent criminal defense attorney's creative posttrial motion resulted in total victory.

Sentencing and Appeal

Sentencing and appeal occur after a jury convicts the defendant.

The excellent criminal defense attorney views sentencing as an opportunity to help the defendant.

After sentence is imposed, the excellent criminal defense attorney always appeals to higher courts.

"We always appeal. Anything can happen!"

— Frank E. Haddad, Jr.,
former President of the National
Association of Criminal
Defense Lawyers

Secret 69 of Criminal Defense

In the event that a defendant is found guilty by the jury and comes before the judge for sentencing, the excellent criminal defense attorney hires a sentencing expert to present the best possible case to the court for leniency.

The sentencing expert interviews the defendant, studies the circumstances of the charges against the defendant, studies the prosecution's theory and evidence against the defendant, studies and evaluates the verdict, and studies and evaluates potential sentencing options available in terms of incarceration, probation, fines, and restitution, and makes a clear, plausible defense-oriented recommendation.

The sentencing expert presents important insights and details to the court to convince the judge to impose a lesser sentence of incarceration, if any, and a smaller fine and restitution, if any.

Secret 70 of Criminal Defense

The excellent criminal defense attorney doesn't need a sentencing expert in some cases.

For instance, an entertainer — the lead singer in one of the hottest international groups — pours vodka on a carpet and sets it afire in his hotel, damages property, and is charged with criminal mischief. The crime charged is minor. The defendant's celebrity status is tremendous.

Nobody wants to punish this defendant. The prosecutor's children have posters of him on the walls of their rooms. The judge dismisses the charges when the entertainer agrees to make public service announcements about fire safety.

Secret 71 of Criminal Defense

In the event that the defendant is convicted by the jury and sentenced by the judge, the excellent criminal defense attorney always appeals to a higher court.

The appellate court may look at all the evidence introduced at trial and conclude there was insufficient evidence as a matter of law to support a verdict of guilty. When the court of appeals reverses a conviction on the grounds of insufficient evidence, the case cannot be brought to trial again. The court of appeals in effect acquits the defendant.

Even if the appellate court doesn't find insufficient evidence, it can reverse the conviction based on trial error and order a new trial. Retrial provides the excellent criminal defense attorney another opportunity to achieve total victory.

Secret 72 of Criminal Defense

In the event that all appeals fail, including appeals from postconviction collateral attacks, the excellent criminal defense attorney seeks to obtain a pardon for his client from the governor or from the President of the United States.

Relationships

The excellent criminal defense attorney's personality plays a major role in his trial practice. He enjoys the people he works with — the prosecutors, the police, the judges, and all the courtroom personnel.

Prosecutors like to try a case against him. A prosecutor says, "They just don't get any better than him. He's smooth as silk. He puts everybody at ease. I want to learn from that. I want to be as good as him."

Judges say, "He is the best criminal lawyer I've ever seen. He's highly informed on the law and prepares the best cases of any lawyer I've ever seen. When he walks into court, he knows every possible fact in the case. There's no trickery whatsoever. His technique is being prepared."

The excellent criminal defense attorney works the legal and political sides of prosecutors, police, and judges over the years, and is so prepared, so likable, and so willing to help that his words and actions achieve maximum effect.

He represents courthouse allies and adversaries alike. He says, "I defend people charged with crime, instead of tying tin cans to their tails."

"Create some goodwill."

— Frank E. Haddad, Jr.,
former President of the National
Association of Criminal
Defense Lawyers

Secret 73 of Criminal Defense

As the years go by, the excellent criminal defense attorney befriends prosecutors. Although the adversarial system creates opportunities for sharp differences in particular cases, the attorney and prosecutors work together within the framework of the criminal justice system. They share that common experience.

The excellent criminal defense attorney treats prosecutors respectfully, with sincerity, and with strength and candor in the defense of a case, both in informal meetings and in the courtroom.

A prosecutor may ask the attorney to contribute a donation to his re-election campaign. The attorney offers substantial donations and assistance, and may even serve as campaign chairman for the prosecutor.

The excellent attorney says, "You know, I've conquered a lot of prosecutors in my practice of criminal defense. I've got a lot of notches on my gun, where I've killed these prosecutors — with kindness. We're friends now, and I'm proud of that achievement."

Secret 74 of Criminal Defense

Sometimes a prosecutor says, "I'm going to put your client in jail and take away everything he enjoys."

The excellent criminal defense attorney says, "I'm going to represent this defendant and dismiss this criminal charge, or obtain acquittal at trial. I will obtain justice for this defendant."

Trials are hard fought. But the excellent criminal defense attorney treats the prosecutor with respect and avoids being angry and distrustful of the prosecutor, even when provoked. He knows the principle: "Reasonable men may disagree."

Secret 75 of Criminal Defense

The excellent criminal defense attorney knows that police officers have legal problems like everybody else. They may need representation in a divorce case, or an accident case. They may want to start a business. The excellent criminal defense attorney discusses these matters with them. He is their friend. Sometimes, a policeman gets into the wrong end of a criminal case. The excellent criminal defense attorney represents him, all the way to acquittal.

The excellent criminal defense attorney understands that a police officer on the street or at headquarters, or in the police evidence and property room, may be able to provide information or evidence helpful in the defense of a criminal case.

Secret 76 of Criminal Defense

The excellent criminal defense attorney befriends judges as well as prosecutors. He knows these judges from law school, and he practices in front of them on a daily basis. Many judges are former prosecutors.

The attorney treats judges with respect and sincerity. He is well prepared when he stands before a judge arguing a case or presenting evidence. He does not waste the court's time.

Judges are human beings. They serve on the bench for many years. Often, these judges stand for reelection. A judge may ask the attorney for a campaign donation or to be his campaign manager. The excellent criminal defense attorney supports the judge's campaign. He creates goodwill with judges.

Secret 77 of Criminal Defense

Bailiffs in state and federal courts are tough as nails. They've seen everything. They handle difficult situations in the courtroom.

They do more than just say, "Hear ye, hear ye. Court is now in session, the honorable Judge John Smith presiding. Come forward all ye who have business in this courtroom, and ye shall be heard. Silence is commanded in the courtroom."

If a defendant gets out of hand, these bailiffs promptly restore order. If onlookers in the courtroom get out of line, these bailiffs restore order.

Bailiffs work for the court. They know what the judge is thinking. Sometimes, a bailiff shares this information with the excellent criminal defense attorney. A bailiff is a good friend to the attorney in a long trial.

Secret 78 of Criminal Defense

The excellent criminal defense attorney treats court reporters with great respect. The court reporter prepares accurate transcripts of trial testimony on a daily basis, or after the entire trial ends. During trial, the court reporter may be asked to read the answer a witness gave earlier in the trial.

The attorney respectfully requests the court reporter to prepare transcripts as needed. He creates goodwill by paying court reporters' fees promptly. The attorney and court reporters enjoy an ongoing, respectful, friendly relationship developed over the course of many, many trials.

Secret 79 of Criminal Defense

The excellent criminal defense attorney establishes a friendly working relationship with court clerks.

Court clerks are the record keepers. They maintain complete files of every case, including transcripts of testimony, all the evidence, and all the motions, responses, and rulings in every case. They maintain and safeguard the integrity of court records and make them available to the attorney.

Secret 80 of Criminal Defense

The excellent criminal defense attorney encourages the public perception that when he gets into a case anything can happen, that he can "turn a green hand," that he can make the lesser argument defeat the greater, that he can make something out of nothing.

He's fun to be around. He's fun to watch. He was born self-confident, and people around him become more self-confident by association. He spontaneously does the right thing. People marvel at his quickness and clever tactics. They admire his readiness to help his fellow man.

Office Practice and Associates

The excellent criminal defense attorney gathers office associates who maximize his chances for total victory — his receptionist, his personal secretary, his bookkeeper, his legal researcher and writer, his investigator, and other attorneys who assist him.

These office associates help develop his cases. The excellent criminal defense attorney relies on them to learn information favorable to the client, to investigate the prosecution's incorrect conclusions, and to create motions to dismiss to torpedo the indictment.

"Once I decide to take a case, I have only one agenda: I want to win. I will try, by every fair and legal means, to get my client off — without regard to the consequences."

— Alan M. Dershowitz,
The Best Defense

Secret 81 of Criminal Defense

The excellent criminal defense attorney relies on his investigator, who locates facts and witnesses, and develops them, which the criminal defense attorney transforms into credible, effective evidence at trial.

The attorney does not hesitate to call on his investigator to testify as a witness, when necessary.

Secret 82 of Criminal Defense

The excellent criminal defense attorney periodically checks his communication devices and offices for eavesdropping invasions. He knows that state and federal law enforcement agencies and media investigators occasionally operate outside the law to gain information to unfairly publicize or ambush a defendant and his attorney.

Secret 83 of Criminal Defense

The excellent criminal defense attorney understands DNA evidence is so scientifically reliable that it trumps traditional identification evidence. He increasingly replaces mistaken eyewitness identification, the single greatest cause of conviction of the innocent, with the certainty of DNA evidence.

DNA evidence first captured the public's confidence and achieved legal acceptance in the O.J. Simpson trial in 1995 when DNA forensic pioneers Barry Scheck and Henry Lee appeared on behalf of Mr. Simpson in such a way that the jurors and the public grasped the significance of DNA evidence.

The excellent criminal defense attorney stays current about DNA developments. He keeps a DNA expert handy, ready to conduct scientific examinations and tests on behalf of his client.

Secret 84 of Criminal Defense

The excellent criminal defense attorney knows the single best reference book summarizing criminal defense law and procedure is the *Annual Review of Criminal Procedure* volume of *The Georgetown Law Journal*, available from The Georgetown Law Journal Association, 600 New Jersey Avenue, N.W., Washington, DC 20001. This authoritative book covers every important aspect of criminal law and procedure currently practiced in America. Every sentence in this book is supported by citations to case law, statutes, or rules.

Representation and Fees

From the time he is retained, the excellent criminal defense attorney works the case. He sticks by the defendant. He says, "I never drop a client. I always keep on trying to help him."

In every case, the excellent criminal defense attorney projects the understanding that he will never betray the client's confidences. In *Taylor v. Blacklow*, 132 *English Reports*, 401, 406 (C.P. 1836), the court stated, "The first duty of an attorney is to keep the secrets of his client."

"Anyone deserves to be helped."

— Frank E. Haddad, Jr.,
   former President of the National
   Association of Criminal
   Defense Lawyers

Secret 85 of Criminal Defense

The excellent criminal defense attorney protects the defendant from prosecutorial misconduct, guarantees the trial is conducted fairly, and assures that the defendant is not convicted in the absence of proof of guilt beyond a reasonable doubt.

The attorney investigates, develops, and presents the defendant's evidence in the light most favorable to the defendant. In the adversary system, it is not the defense attorney's duty to determine guilt or innocence, which is up to the jury. In advocating the defendant's theory of defense, the defense attorney pursues every avenue of defense within the laws and rules of practice.

Secret 86 of Criminal Defense

The excellent criminal defense attorney knows that rule number one regarding fees for the defense of a criminal case is to receive the fee in full up front. He says, "It doesn't pay to open the store unless you ring the register."

Secret 87 of Criminal Defense

The excellent criminal defense attorney charges the fee he is comfortable with. His fee is based on his idea of how much work is involved, and how much difficulty is involved, in defending a particular defendant. He knows he will be working not only to win the case, but also to restore the defendant's sense of balance, which is priceless.

He is the attorney to retain without regard to cost.

Secret 88 of Criminal Defense

The excellent criminal defense attorney's fee includes his services and the services of his entire office, including his receptionist, his secretaries, his law clerks, and his library. He keeps his library and databases current. His fee includes all his support staff and resources.

In the event that the excellent criminal defense attorney decides that outside assistance is necessary, the client pays for it.

Secret 89 of Criminal Defense

The excellent criminal defense attorney who has mastered the criminal defense profession is in such demand that he must charge high fees to protect his time and private life.

The situation is different with a beginning lawyer starting out, who aspires to achieve mastery of the criminal defense profession. In those first months, the beginning criminal defense attorney goes to the courthouse and offers his services for free to represent defendants. There he learns the ropes of jury practice, argues points of law in a courtroom, manages defendants and prosecutors, and educates juries. Nothing can replace this experience.

When the beginning criminal defense attorney starts to win cases, here come the clients with money.

The Criminal Defense Attorney Tradition

A young lawyer fresh out of law school understudied an established, excellent criminal defense attorney, and thereby learned skills and techniques from the best. The older lawyer shared techniques not learned in law school.

> Oh, he was great. In those days, there might be 300 to 400 people in the criminal courtroom to hear him give a final argument. He was a powerful, passionate man, good at quoting the Bible. I remember one time he talked for 90 minutes and had the jury in the palm of his hand the whole time. He was the best.

The young lawyer developed into an excellent criminal defense attorney — one of the greatest.

> The vast majority of my work comes from middle-class people. By the same token, I represent people from all walks of life. I enjoy it. It's a great education, seeing how people react, how predicaments affect them, and their lives, how they regroup. I get great satisfaction out of doing a great job for them.

The excellent criminal defense attorney works tirelessly, fearlessly, and creatively for his clients. From thousands of lawyers, he emerges alone on a summit so high that few come near it.

> I tell you, the pressure of the responsibility — having a man's liberty, or even his life, dependent on your ability — is tremendous. It's pressure that some lawyers can't take. They try a criminal case, it breaks them, and they go back to civil law and stay there.

The excellent criminal defense attorney has stamina and drive for the practice of criminal defense.

"I have practiced law for forty years, and I've loved every minute of it."

— Johnnie Cochran, Los Angeles, one of the greatest criminal defense attorneys of all time

Secret 90 of Criminal Defense

The excellent criminal defense attorney joins as many professional organizations as time allows. These include local, state, and federal bar associations, and local, state, and national criminal defense lawyer organizations. He becomes a leader in these organizations, whose members share a wealth of information, tactics, and criminal practice skills.

He takes time to educate beginning criminal defense attorneys on their way to achieving mastery of the criminal defense practice, in person, in presentations, and in articles.

Secret 91 of Criminal Defense

In law school, the student learns about the criminal laws, the rules of criminal procedure, the rules of evidence, and the rules of appellate procedure. He reads hundreds of cases, especially decisions of the United States Supreme Court.

He learns about fundamental principles of the criminal justice system in America. He learns enough to graduate and pass the bar examination. When he receives his license to practice law, he is ready to begin the journey to become an excellent criminal defense attorney.

Secret 92 of Criminal Defense

As soon as he receives his license to practice law, the beginning lawyer is authorized to go to trial on behalf of a criminal defendant. There's no waiting period. "Jump right in."

Secret 93 of Criminal Defense

The beginning lawyer develops full mastery of criminal defense practice in two ways: 1) apprenticeship with an established master of criminal defense practice, and 2) work in volume.

Secret 94 of Criminal Defense

Earl Rogers of Los Angeles, California was one of the great heroes among excellent criminal defense attorneys. Rogers advertised his motto, "Call us and keep your mouth shut." He won acquittals by thorough study of facts and testimony; he found overlooked witnesses and evidence. *Final Verdict* is an excellent biography of Earl Rogers.

A generation of excellent criminal defense attorneys flourished in the second half of the twentieth century, including Edward Bennett Williams of Washington, DC, Henry Rothblatt of New York City, Richard "Racehorse" Haynes of Houston, Texas, Gerry Spence of Wyoming, and F. Lee Bailey of Massachusetts and Florida. Two other excellent criminal defense trial attorneys in recent times were Frank Haddad of Louisville, Kentucky, and James F. Neal of Nashville, Tennessee. The incomparable Johnnie Cochran won acquittal for his client O.J. Simpson in perhaps the most celebrated trial in the history of criminal defense. Alan M. Dershowitz of Cambridge, Massachusetts periodically astonishes the legal world with astounding results in high-profile cases.

Beginning criminal defense attorneys learn much from these and other excellent criminal defense attorneys, who share secrets of criminal defense neither known nor taught in law school.

Secret 95 of Criminal Defense

Some excellent criminal defense attorneys are former prosecutors with extensive trial experience, who have finally seen the light and joined the defense side, bringing their own bags of tricks with them. They achieve a high percentage of acquittals. These former prosecutors tell jurors straight out, "Ladies and gentlemen, I served as first assistant district attorney for twenty years, and I can tell you with absolute certainty, that every police officer who testifies at trial does not tell the whole truth."

Beginning criminal defense attorneys learn much from these former prosecutors who have become excellent criminal defense attorneys.

Secret 96 of Criminal Defense

The beginning criminal defense attorney pursues work in volume, exhaustive preparation, and the guidance of an excellent criminal defense attorney.

On the way to achieving the highest level of mastery in the practice of criminal defense, the beginning criminal defense attorney who makes a mistake takes heart in the maxim, "Live and learn."

Secret 97 of Criminal Defense

Many lawyers try a few criminal cases in their careers, but only a small percentage of lawyers become criminal defense attorneys. And only a very small percentage of criminal defense attorneys become excellent criminal defense attorneys.

Ethics

The United States Supreme Court confirms the excellent criminal defense attorney's goal of total victory.

> [W]e insist that [defense counsel] defend his client whether he is innocent or guilty. The State has the obligation to present the evidence. Defense counsel need present nothing, even if he knows what the truth is. He need not furnish any witnesses to the police, or reveal any confidences of his client, or furnish any other information to help the prosecution's case. If he can confuse a witness, even a truthful one, or make him appear at a disadvantage, unsure or indecisive, that will be his normal course. Our interest in not convicting the innocent permits counsel to put the State to its proof, to put the State's case in the worst possible light, regardless of what he thinks or knows to be the truth. Justice Byron White, *United States v. Wade*, 388 U.S. 218, 257-258 (1967).

This ethical mandate, and the commitment to never betray confidential information given by his client, guides the excellent criminal defense attorney's quest to total victory — acquittal after acquittal.

"My clients know I will hold the lantern for them."

— Frank E. Haddad, Jr.,
former President of the National
Association of Criminal
Defense Lawyers

Secret 98 of Criminal Defense

It is not the responsibility of the excellent criminal defense attorney to determine the legal guilt or innocence of his client. The jury decides guilt or innocence.

In every case, the excellent criminal defense attorney works to win. He does everything he can think of, within the law and the rules, to achieve the total victory of acquittal, or the dismissal of the indictment, or reversal on appeal.

He mounts every conceivable defense to convince the jury to vote for acquittal. He attacks the prosecutor's case in every way possible to limit the prosecutor's evidence, to exclude the prosecutor's evidence, to discredit the prosecutor's evidence, to destroy the case of the government against the accused. The attorney requires the prosecutor to prove the defendant's guilt as charged beyond a reasonable doubt, in a trial fairly conducted.

The excellent criminal defense attorney is confident he will win. He wins because he is more experienced and more knowledgeable than the prosecutor; his presentation is more convincing.

Secret 99 of Criminal Defense

The excellent criminal defense attorney never loses a case defending someone he feels is innocent.

There are so many opportunities in the criminal process to win a case. Somewhere along the line, the attorney is successful. There are so many opportunities. He persistently works the case until he gets the break he is looking for. Then he develops it into total victory.

Secret 100 of Criminal Defense

The excellent criminal defense attorney never loses any case, because, in every case, he does everything he can think of, within the law and the rules, to win.

Because he gives everything, how can he lose?